LITTLE TREATS
cookies

Elinor Klivans

Illustrations by Clarisse Tanjo

TABLE OF CONTENTS

PIPED COOKIES

ROLLED AND CUT COOKIES

BROWNIES AND BARS

COOKIE TIME

From chewy chocolate chip cookies to sophisticated almond-filled macaroons to fudgy brownies slathered with chocolate frosting, cookies, brownies, and bars suit any occasion. Sturdier drop cookies are ideal for filling a picnic basket or tucking into lunch boxes, while delicate, cream-filled lace cookies and macaroons are classic tea party treats. Many of the treats in this book make festive gifts for everyone on your list when nestled into holiday tins.

types of cookies

The most basic of styles, drop cookies are formed by simply spooning mounds of soft dough onto a baking sheet. Many all-time favorites, such as chocolate chip cookies, are part of this group. Shaped cookies, a slightly more involved type, come in many forms. They can be rolled or formed by hand, piped through a pastry bag, or extruded through a cookie press. Sturdy doughs that can be rolled out thinly, cut into shapes using cookie cutters or a knife, and baked without losing their shape are best for making rolled and cut cookies. Brownies and bars, although similar to cookies in mixing and in final texture, start as batters that are poured or spread into a pan and can be cut into perfectly-sized individual servings after they bake.

readying your supplies

Several hours before baking, check the recipe to see if butter, cream cheese, or other ingredients need to be brought to room temperature before use. Remember to turn the oven on at least 20 minutes ahead of time so that it reaches the proper temperature by the time you're ready to bake. Before you begin, assemble and prepare all of the equipment and ingredients needed for the recipe. This includes sifting dry ingredients, squeezing juices, grating citrus zest, chopping chocolate, and, of course, measuring everything carefully. Place the ingredients easily within reach, preferably in the order that they will be added so you can be sure that nothing has been left out of the mixture.

mixing doughs & batters

Preparing cookie dough often begins with creaming the butter and sugar together until the color changes from soft yellow to cream. This yields a light, fluffy mixture that combines well with the remaining ingredients and helps to create a tender texture. When creaming, it is important that the butter be at room temperature; if it is too cold, it's difficult to aerate, and if it is too warm, the mixture will be dense. An electric mixer is the most efficient tool for creaming, although it can also be done by hand with a wooden spoon.

Next, add eggs and flavorings such as citrus juice, extracts, spices, or melted chocolate.

Cold eggs can cause the bits of butter to harden, giving the mixture a slightly curdled look. If this happens, don't be concerned: adding the dry ingredients will return the dough to a smooth consistency. Be sure to pour in the dry ingredients slowly and mix them in at a low speed to avoid a mess on the countertop. Finally, stir in any ingredients used to stud the dough or batter with additional flavor, such as nuts, dried fruits, or chocolate chips.

If a recipe calls for separated eggs, start with eggs straight from the refrigerator—cold eggs are easier to separate. If you need to whip the whites, let them come to room temperature before beating. Be sure that no yolks get into the whites, as this will prevent them from whipping properly. Store any unused yolks for another recipe.

To fold a light mixture (such as beaten egg whites) into a heavier mixture, begin by piling one-third of the lighter mixture on top of the heavier mixture. Using a rubber spatula held vertically, slice down through the center of the mixtures to the bottom of the bowl. Turn the spatula horizontally, so it lies on the bottom of the bowl, and pull it along the bottom and up the side of the bowl, keeping the spatula flat. Pull the spatula up and over the lighter mixture, bringing some of the heavier mixture from the bottom with it. Rotate the bowl a quarter turn and repeat the folding action. Continue the folding action, rotating the bowl each time, until no white streaks remain. Once the batter has lightened in color, fold in the rest of the lighter mixture.

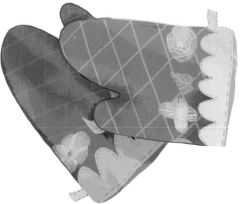

monitoring your oven

If your oven does not seem to be heating properly, use an oven thermometer, which can be kept in the oven at all times, to check the oven's accuracy. If the temperature is slightly off, you can adjust the temperature control knob up or down until the oven reaches the correct temperature. If there is a serious discrepancy, you should have the oven checked and recalibrated by a professional. Small pockets of higher heat, called "hot spots," can occur in any oven. To compensate for them and ensure even baking, bake cookies and brownies on the middle rack of the oven, one sheet at a time.

Convection ovens (gas or electric) have an internal fan that helps circulate air during baking in order to produce even heat all over the oven. With a convection oven, two baking sheets of cookies can be baked evenly at the same time, but convection ovens bake more quickly than standard ovens so baking times and temperatures will need adjustment.

Since individual ovens can vary, times given in the recipes are approximate guidelines. Therefore, it is important to check cookies, brownies, and bars often as they near the end of the recommended baking time.

serving your treats

Proper cooling and the right tools are all you need for presenting these help-yourself sweets. Stock your kitchen with a variety of spatulas for transferring cookies of all sizes from the cookie sheets, wire racks for cooling, and a sharp knife to cut finished bars and brownies into individual servings.

Most cookies, brownies, and bars are served at room temperature for best flavor and texture, but there are some exceptions. For example, Tangy Lemon Bars (page 91) and similar treats become too soft at room temperature, so they are best served cold, straight from the refrigerator. Frosted Chocolate Brownies (page 100) should be stored in the refrigerator to keep the frosting in the best condition, and Blueberry Cheesecake Bars (page 96) must be refrigerated in order to keep them fresh.

Although cookies, brownies, and bars, simply stacked on a platter, make a lovely presentation, some additional planning can add to their

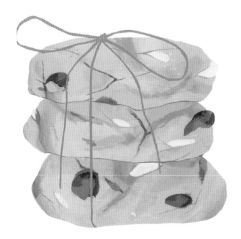

appeal. Think about complementary shapes and colors when deciding to arrange and serve an assortment of treats. Arrange bars and brownies neatly on a large plate, create appealing piles of rustic cookies, or spaciously arrange more delicate or decorative treats. Use flat platters or plates to prevent cookies from sliding around too much. For a casual barbecue or picnic, line a basket with a colorful napkin and fill it with portable cookies that won't break. For parties, serve cookies, brownies, or bars on several small, decorative plates placed in different locations around the room. It's a good idea to cut bars into small pieces so guests can sample different types. Plan to serve two to three cookies, brownies, or bars per person, remembering that some people will want to try several kinds.

The best storage containers are metal tins or plastic containers that can be sealed tightly. Sticky or frosted cookies, brownies, and bars are best stored in single layers. Other cookies can be layered in the container between sheets of waxed paper. To keep baked goods in prime condition for serving, always store them in the recommended containers and keep them at the correct temperature.

In pretty packaging, cookies, brownies, and bars are welcome gifts for any occasion. Keep a selection of decorative tins on hand to line with waxed paper and fill with cookies; or fill small plastic bags about three-quarters full and tie them with ribbons and tags, or seal them with stickers. Beautiful gift boxes lined with waxed paper can hold an assortment of cookies, brownies, or bars. For more about packing and shipping baked goods, see page 109.

baking tips

Although cookies, brownies, and bars can be simple to prepare, it is still important to keep in mind a few key things to ensure perfect results for all baked goods.

- Use fresh ingredients and be sure they are at the proper temperatures.

- Use liquid measuring cups for liquids and dry measuring cups for dry ingredients. Measuring spoons can be used for both types of ingredients.

- Use the "spoon and sweep" method for measuring dry ingredients: Use a spoon to fill the cup to overflowing and then level the top with a knife.

- When measuring sticky ingredients such as honey or molasses, oil the measuring cup or spoon first so the thick liquid will slide out easily.

- Keep your measuring tools well organized and clean them for reuse as you go.

- Stay attentive during the baking process, watching that the cookies don't get too brown.

- To ensure cookies stay crisp, cool them on wire racks; this allows the air to circulate evenly around the entire surface of the cookies.

- If you live in a high-altitude area, check with your local agricultural extension office for information on standard baking conversions.

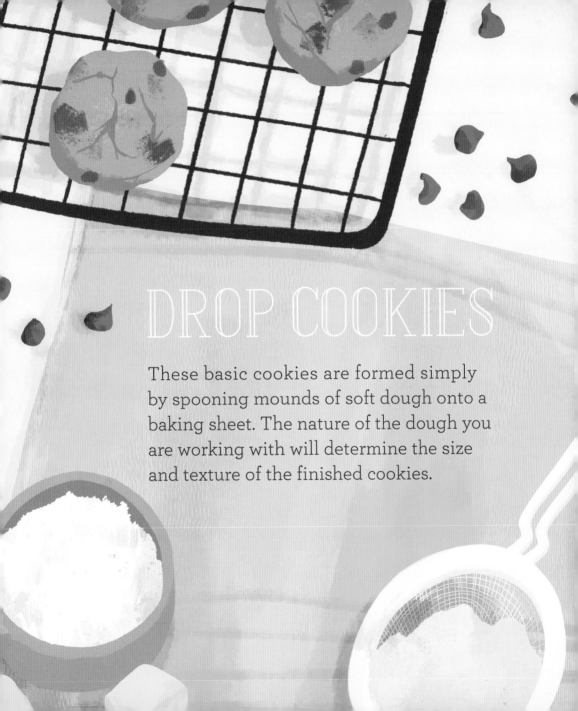

DROP COOKIES

These basic cookies are formed simply by spooning mounds of soft dough onto a baking sheet. The nature of the dough you are working with will determine the size and texture of the finished cookies.

PEANUT BUTTER COOKIES

Baking these cookies will satisfy the fans of both creamy and crunchy peanut butter: The insides have a soft, chewy texture and the outsides are topped with crisp chopped roasted nuts.

2 cups all-purpose flour

1 teaspoon baking soda

½ teaspoon salt

½ cup unsalted butter, at room temperature

½ cup smooth peanut butter, at room temperature

⅔ cup firmly packed dark brown sugar

½ cup granulated sugar

2 large eggs

1 teaspoon vanilla extract

⅓ cup coarsely chopped unsalted roasted peanuts

MAKES 26 COOKIES

1 Position a rack in the middle of the oven and preheat to 350°F. Line 2 large cookie sheets with parchment paper.

2 In a bowl, sift together the flour, baking soda, and salt; set aside. In a large bowl, combine the butter, peanut butter, brown sugar, and granulated sugar. Using a mixer on medium speed, beat until well blended, about 1 minute. Add the eggs and vanilla and beat on low speed until the eggs are completely incorporated, scraping down the bowl occasionally with a rubber spatula. Slowly add the flour mixture and beat on low speed just until incorporated.

3 Place heaping tablespoonfuls of the dough 3 inches apart on the prepared cookie sheets. Sprinkle about ½ teaspoon of the chopped peanuts over each cookie, pressing lightly with your fingertips to help them adhere. Bake, 1 sheet at a time, until the cookie tops are evenly golden, 10–12 minutes.

4 Let the cookies cool on the cookie sheet for 5 minutes, then, using a wide metal spatula, transfer to wire racks to cool completely, about 30 minutes. Repeat to bake and cool the remaining cookies. Store the cookies in an airtight container at room temperature for up to 3 days.

CHEWY COCONUT MACAROONS

The key to making light and moist macaroons is first to stir the batter to separate and distribute the shreds of coconut, then beat the egg whites to soft peaks and fold them gently into the dough.

1 Position a rack in the middle of the oven and preheat to 325°F. Line 2 large cookie sheets with parchment paper and butter the paper.

2 In a large bowl, using a fork, stir together the coconut, condensed milk, salt, and vanilla and almond extracts until well blended; set aside. In a clean, large bowl, combine the egg whites and cream of tartar. Using a mixer on medium speed, beat until the egg whites are foamy, about 1 minute. Increase the speed to medium-high and continue beating until the egg whites look shiny and smooth and form soft peaks, 2–3 minutes. Slowly add the sugar and beat until stiff peaks form in the egg whites, about 1 minute longer. Using a rubber spatula, in 2 batches, gently fold the egg whites into the coconut mixture until no white streaks remain.

3 Place rounded tablespoonfuls of the dough 1½ inches apart on the prepared cookie sheets. Bake, 1 sheet at a time, until the cookie edges and some tips of the coconut shreds are lightly browned, 15–17 minutes.

4 Let the cookies cool on the cookie sheet for 5 minutes, then, using a wide metal spatula, transfer to wire racks to cool completely, about 30 minutes. Repeat to bake and cool the remaining cookies. Store in an airtight container at room temperature for up to 3 days.

14 ounces sweetened shredded coconut

1 cup sweetened condensed milk

¼ teaspoon salt

1 teaspoon vanilla extract

2 teaspoons almond extract

4 large egg whites

¼ teaspoon cream of tartar

2 tablespoons granulated sugar

MAKES 36 COOKIES

CHOCOLATE CHIP
COOKIE SANDWICHES

A thick layer of chocolate frosting in the middle of two classic chocolate chip cookies creates a treat no chocolate lover can resist. The cookies are also good on their own, without the frosting.

2 cups all-purpose flour

1 teaspoon baking soda

½ teaspoon salt

1 cup unsalted butter, at room temperature

¾ cup firmly packed light brown sugar

¾ cup granulated sugar

2 large eggs, cold

2 teaspoons vanilla extract

2 cups semisweet chocolate chips

Chocolate Frosting, page 89

MAKES 32 COOKIES

1 Position a rack in the middle of the oven and preheat to 350°F. Line 3 large cookie sheets with parchment paper.

2 In a bowl, sift together the flour, baking soda, and salt; set aside. In a large bowl, combine the butter, brown sugar, and granulated sugar. Using a mixer on medium speed, beat until well blended, about 1 minute. Add the eggs and vanilla and beat on low speed until the eggs are completely incorporated, scraping down the bowl occasionally with a rubber spatula. Slowly add the flour mixture and beat on low speed just until incorporated. Add the chocolate chips and beat just until distributed.

3 Place heaping tablespoonfuls of the dough 3 inches apart on the prepared cookie sheets. Bake, 1 sheet at a time, until the cookie tops are lightly golden in the center, 10–12 minutes.

4 Let the cookies cool on the cookie sheet for 5 minutes, then, using a wide metal spatula, transfer to wire racks to cool completely, about 30 minutes. Repeat to bake and cool the remaining cookies. Store the cookies in an airtight container at room temperature for up to 3 days.

5 To assemble, turn half of the cookies bottom side up. Use an
icing spatula to spread a thick layer of frosting over each cookie
bottom. Gently press the remaining cookies, bottom side down, onto
the filling. Serve right away.

OATMEAL-RAISIN CRISPS

These classic goodies offer the pleasing consistency of crisp cookies studded with plenty of chewy raisins. For the right texture, be sure to use old-fashioned rolled oats, not the quick-cooking kind.

1 Position a rack in the middle of the oven and preheat to 350°F. Line 3 large cookie sheets with parchment paper.

2 In a bowl, sift together the flour, baking soda, baking powder, cinnamon, and salt; set aside. In a large bowl, combine the butter, brown sugar, and granulated sugar. Using a mixer on medium speed, beat until well blended, about 1 minute. Add the eggs and vanilla and beat on low speed until the eggs are completely incorporated, scraping down the bowl occasionally with a rubber spatula. Slowly add the flour mixture and beat on low speed just until incorporated. Add the oats and raisins and beat until incorporated.

3 Place heaping tablespoonfuls of the dough 2½ inches apart on the prepared cookie sheets. Bake, 1 sheet at a time, until the cookie tops are evenly golden, 11–14 minutes.

4 Let the cookies cool on the cookie sheet for 5 minutes, then, using a wide metal spatula, transfer to wire racks to cool completely, about 30 minutes. Repeat to bake and cool the remaining cookies. Store the cookies in an airtight container at room temperature for up to 3 days.

2 cups all-purpose flour

1 teaspoon baking soda

¾ teaspoon baking powder

1½ teaspoons ground cinnamon

½ teaspoon salt

1 cup unsalted butter, at room temperature

1 cup firmly packed light brown sugar

1 cup granulated sugar

2 large eggs

2 teaspoons vanilla extract

2½ cups old-fashioned rolled oats

2 cups raisins

MAKES 40 COOKIES

WHITE CHOCOLATE-MACADAMIA COOKIES

This light, tasty cookie, a bakery favorite, has an appealing tropical crunch. For the best flavor, be sure to use unsalted macadamia nuts and look for white chocolate chips that contain cocoa butter.

2 cups all-purpose flour

1 teaspoon baking soda

½ teaspoon salt

1 cup unsalted butter, at room temperature

¾ cup firmly packed light brown sugar

¾ cup granulated sugar

2 large eggs, cold

2 teaspoons vanilla extract

2 cups white chocolate chips

¾ cup coarsely chopped unsalted roasted macadamia nuts

MAKES 32 COOKIES

1 Position a rack in the middle of the oven and preheat to 350°F. Line 3 large cookie sheets with parchment paper.

2 In a bowl, sift together the flour, baking soda, and salt; set aside. In a large bowl, combine the butter, brown sugar, and granulated sugar. Using a mixer on medium speed, beat until well blended, about 1 minute. Add the eggs and vanilla and beat on low speed until the eggs are completely incorporated, scraping down the bowl occasionally with a rubber spatula. Slowly add the flour mixture and beat on low speed just until incorporated. Add the white chocolate chips and nuts and beat just until distributed.

3 Place heaping tablespoonfuls of the dough 3 inches apart on the prepared cookie sheets. Bake, 1 sheet at a time, until the cookie tops are lightly golden in the center, 10–12 minutes.

4 Let the cookies cool on the cookie sheet for 5 minutes, then, using a wide metal spatula, transfer to wire racks to cool completely, about 30 minutes. Repeat to bake and cool the remaining cookies. Store the cookies in an airtight container at room temperature for up to 3 days.

TRIPLE-CHOCOLATE-CHUNK COOKIES

Chopped chunks of dark, milk, and white chocolate stud these cookies with a variety of colors and flavors. When baked, the chocolate chunks melt into pleasing, irregularly shaped pieces.

1 Position a rack in the middle of the oven and preheat to 350°F. Line 3 large cookie sheets with parchment paper.

2 In a bowl, sift together the flour, baking soda, and salt; set aside. In a large bowl, combine the butter, brown sugar, and granulated sugar. Using a mixer on medium speed, beat until well blended, about 1 minute. Add the eggs and vanilla and beat on low speed until the eggs are completely incorporated, scraping down the bowl occasionally with a rubber spatula. Slowly add the flour mixture and beat on low speed just until incorporated. Add the chopped chocolate and beat just until distributed.

3 Place heaping tablespoonfuls of the dough 3 inches apart on the prepared cookie sheets. Bake, 1 sheet at a time, until the cookie tops are lightly golden in the center, 10–12 minutes.

4 Let the cookies cool on the cookie sheet for 5 minutes, then, using a wide metal spatula, transfer to wire racks to cool completely, about 30 minutes. Repeat to bake and cool the remaining cookies. Store the cookies in an airtight container at room temperature for up to 3 days.

2 cups all-purpose flour

1 teaspoon baking soda

½ teaspoon salt

1 cup unsalted butter, at room temperature

¾ cup firmly packed light brown sugar

¾ cup granulated sugar

2 large eggs, cold

2 teaspoons vanilla extract

¾ cup chopped (¼–½-inch pieces) semisweet chocolate

¾ cup chopped (¼–½-inch pieces) milk chocolate

¾ cup chopped (¼–½-inch pieces) white chocolate

MAKES 32 COOKIES

SHAPED COOKIES

These cookies use a variety of dough-shaping techniques—like pressing with fingertips, rolling between palms, flattening with a rolling pin, and patting by hand—to create distinct forms.

BUTTERY VANILLA SHORTBREAD

A vanilla bean adds its pleasing flavor and aroma to this easy-to-make treat. Be sure to cut the shortbread as soon as it emerges from the oven to ensure that the wedges stay intact.

1 Position a rack in the middle of the oven and preheat to 350°F. Have ready a 9½-inch tart pan with a removable bottom.

2 In a bowl, sift together the flour, cornstarch, and salt; set aside. In a large bowl, combine the butter and sugar. Using a sharp paring knife, cut the vanilla bean pod open lengthwise. Use the tip of the knife to scrape the seeds into the bowl. Using a mixer on medium speed, beat until the mixture is creamy white and smooth, about 4 minutes. Slowly add the flour mixture and beat on low speed just until the dough forms large clumps and pulls away from the sides of the bowl.

3 Using a rubber spatula, spread the dough evenly in the tart pan and smooth the top with an offset spatula. Using a fork, prick the entire surface of the dough, making ¼-inch-deep holes at 1½-inch intervals. Place the tart pan on a cookie sheet and bake until the shortbread center is very lightly golden, 45–50 minutes.

4 Use a sharp knife to cut the warm shortbread into 12 wedges, then let cool in the pan. When ready to serve, remove the pan sides and slide the wedges off the pan bottom. Store the shortbread in an airtight container at room temperature for up to 5 days.

2 cups all-purpose flour

½ cup cornstarch

¼ teaspoon salt

1 cup unsalted butter, at room temperature

½ cup superfine sugar

1 vanilla bean, or 3 teaspoons vanilla extract

MAKES 12 COOKIES

CRUNCHY ESPRESSO SHORTBREAD

Bold coffee flavor accents a simple butter cookie to make the perfect companion for a midday or after-dinner cup of coffee. Look for espresso powder in an Italian deli or gourmet market.

2 cups all-purpose flour

½ cup cornstarch

¼ teaspoon salt

1 cup unsalted butter, at room temperature

½ cup superfine sugar

1 tablespoon instant espresso powder, dissolved in 1 tablespoon water

confectioners' sugar for sprinkling

MAKES 12 COOKIES

1 Position a rack in the middle of the oven and preheat to 350°F. Have ready a 9½-inch tart pan with a removable bottom.

2 In a bowl, sift together the flour, cornstarch, and salt; set aside. In a large bowl, combine the butter and sugar. Using a mixer on medium speed, beat until the mixture is creamy white and smooth, about 4 minutes. Add the dissolved espresso and beat to combine well. Slowly add the flour mixture and beat on low speed just until the dough forms large clumps and pulls away from the sides of the bowl.

3 Using a rubber spatula, spread the dough evenly in the tart pan and smooth the top with an offset spatula. Using a fork, prick the entire surface of the dough, making ¼-inch-deep holes at 1½-inch intervals. Place the tart pan on a cookie sheet and bake until the shortbread center is very lightly golden, 45–50 minutes.

4 Use a sharp knife to cut the warm shortbread into 12 wedges, then let cool in the pan. When ready to serve, remove the pan sides and slide the wedges off the pan bottom. Sift confectioners' sugar evenly over the wedges. Store the shortbread in an airtight container at room temperature for up to 5 days.

FRAGRANT LAVENDER SHORTBREAD

Lavender lends its gentle perfume and soft lemon flavor to these crisp cookies. Purchase delicate fresh lavender flowers from an organic market or dried lavender in jars from a specialty-food store.

1 Position a rack in the middle of the oven and preheat to 350°F. Have ready a 9½-inch tart pan with a removable bottom.

2 In a bowl, sift together the flour, cornstarch, and salt; set aside. In a large bowl, combine the butter and sugar. Using a mixer on medium speed, beat until the mixture is creamy white and smooth, about 4 minutes. Add the lavender and beat to combine well. Slowly add the flour mixture and beat on low speed just until the dough forms large clumps and pulls away from the sides of the bowl.

3 Using a rubber spatula, spread the dough evenly in the tart pan and smooth the top with an offset spatula. Using a fork, prick the entire surface of the dough, making ¼-inch-deep holes at 1½-inch intervals. Place the tart pan on a cookie sheet and bake until the shortbread center is very lightly golden, 45–50 minutes.

4 Use a sharp knife to cut the warm shortbread into 12 wedges, then let cool in the pan. When ready to serve, remove the pan sides and slide the wedges off the pan bottom. Store the shortbread in an airtight container at room temperature for up to 5 days.

2 cups all-purpose flour

½ cup cornstarch

¼ teaspoon salt

1 cup unsalted butter, at room temperature

½ cup superfine sugar

2 tablespoons finely chopped unsprayed fresh or dried lavender flowers

MAKES 12 COOKIES

GOOEY CHOCOLATE CRINKLE COOKIES

These cookies decorate themselves while they bake, the coating of powdered sugar crackling to reveal the fudgelike interiors. A touch of coffee adds complexity to the rich chocolate flavor.

4 tablespoons unsalted butter, at room temperature

4 ounces unsweetened chocolate, chopped

2 ounces semisweet chocolate, chopped

2 cups all-purpose flour

1 teaspoon baking powder

¼ teaspoon salt

4 large eggs

2 cups granulated sugar

1 teaspoon vanilla extract

1 teaspoon instant coffee powder, dissolved in 2 teaspoons water

½ cup confectioners' sugar

MAKES 32 COOKIES

1 In a double boiler insert or a large metal bowl that fits on the rim of a saucepan, combine the butter and chopped chocolates. Place the insert or bowl over, but not touching, barely simmering water. Heat, stirring often, until the chocolates are melted and smooth, 3–4 minutes. Set aside to cool slightly.

2 In a bowl, sift together the flour, baking powder, and salt; set aside. In a large bowl, combine the eggs and granulated sugar. Using a mixer on medium-high speed, beat until pale yellow and thickened, about 2 minutes, scraping down the bowl occasionally with a rubber spatula. Add the vanilla and dissolved coffee and beat until well blended. Slowly add the flour mixture and beat on low speed just until incorporated. Cover and refrigerate for about 2 hours.

3 Position a rack in the middle of the oven and preheat to 325°F. Line 2 large cookie sheets with parchment paper. Sift the confectioners' sugar into a bowl. Scoop up a rounded tablespoonful of the dough, then roll the dough between the palms of your hands into a ball. Lightly roll the dough ball in the sugar to coat it

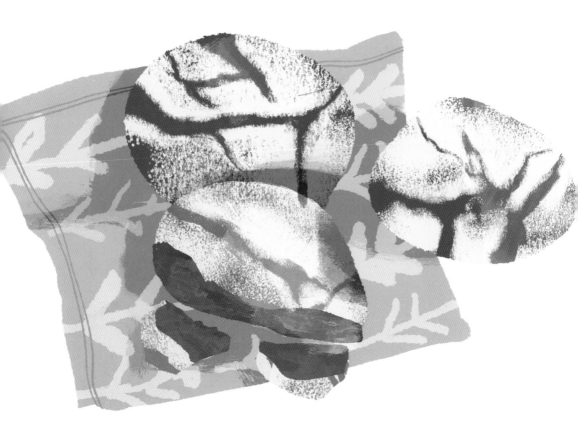

completely and place on a prepared cookie sheet. Repeat with the remaining dough, spacing the dough balls about 2½ inches apart. Bake, 1 sheet at a time, until the cookie tops are puffed, crinkled, and feel firm, 13–15 minutes.

4 Let the cookies cool on the cookie sheet for 5 minutes, then, using a wide metal spatula, transfer to wire racks to cool completely, about 30 minutes. Store the cookies in an airtight container at room temperature for up to 3 days.

SPICY GINGER SNAPS

Although they start out round, during baking these beloved cookies puff up like a hat, then spread into their characteristic flat shape, attractively cracking on the tops.

1 Position a rack in the middle of the oven and preheat to 325°F. Line 2 large cookie sheets with parchment paper.

2 In a bowl, sift together the flour, baking soda, salt, cinnamon, ginger, and cloves; set aside. In a large bowl, combine the butter and the 1 cup sugar. Using a mixer on medium speed, beat until well blended, about 1 minute. Add the egg and molasses and beat on low speed until completely incorporated, scraping down the bowl occasionally with a rubber spatula. Slowly add the flour mixture and beat on low speed just until incorporated.

3 Put the ¼ cup sugar in a small bowl. Scoop up a rounded tablespoonful of the dough, then roll the dough between the palms of your hands into a ball. Lightly roll the dough ball in the sugar to coat it completely and place on a prepared cookie sheet. Repeat with the remaining dough, spacing the dough balls about 3 inches apart. Bake, 1 sheet at a time, until the cookie edges are just lightly browned and the tops are firm at the edges and cracked in the center, 14–16 minutes.

4 Let the cookies cool on the cookie sheet for 5 minutes, then, using a wide metal spatula, transfer to wire racks to cool completely, about 30 minutes. Store the cookies in an airtight container at room temperature for up to 3 days.

2 cups all-purpose flour

1 teaspoon baking soda

¼ teaspoon salt

¾ teaspoon ground cinnamon

1½ teaspoons ground ginger

½ teaspoon ground cloves

¾ cup unsalted butter, at room temperature

1 cup granulated sugar, plus ¼ cup for coating

1 large egg

¼ cup molasses

MAKES 20 COOKIES

MEXICAN WEDDING COOKIES

Ground pecans and butter work together to create the rich flavor and melting texture of these bite-sized balls. Confectioners' sugar coats the baked cookies and adds a sweet finish.

2 cups all-purpose flour

½ teaspoon salt

1½ cups pecans

⅔ cup confectioners' sugar, plus 1 cup for coating

1 cup unsalted butter, at room temperature

2 teaspoons vanilla extract

MAKES 48 COOKIES

1 Position a rack in the middle of the oven and preheat to 325°F. Line 2 large cookie sheets with parchment paper.

2 In a bowl, sift together the flour and salt; set aside. In a food processor, combine the pecans and the ⅔ cup confectioners' sugar. Pulse to chop the nuts coarsely, then process until finely ground, about 2 minutes. In a large bowl, combine the butter, ground pecan mixture, and vanilla. Using a mixer on medium speed, beat until well blended, about 1 minute. Slowly add the flour mixture and beat on low speed just until incorporated.

3 Scoop up a level tablespoonful of the dough. Roll the dough between the palms of your hands into a ball and place it on a prepared cookie sheet. Repeat with the remaining dough, spacing the dough balls 1 inch apart. Bake, 1 sheet at a time, until the cookie tops are lightly browned, 18–20 minutes.

4 Let the cookies cool on the cookie sheet for 5 minutes, then, using a metal spatula, transfer to wire racks to cool completely, about 30 minutes.

5 Sift the 1 cup confectioners' sugar into a shallow bowl. Lightly roll each cooled cookie in the sugar to coat it completely. Store the cookies in an airtight container at room temperature for up to 3 days.

BERRY-PECAN THUMBPRINTS

This is a great recipe to make with kids, who will love pressing their thumb into each cookie to form the indentations. When baked, the jam becomes firm and chewy and the nuts turn toasty.

1 Position a rack in the middle of the oven and preheat to 325°F. Line 1 large cookie sheet with parchment paper.

2 In a bowl, sift together the flour and salt; set aside. In a large bowl, combine the butter and sugar. Using a mixer on medium speed, beat until well blended, about 1 minute. Add the egg yolks and vanilla and beat on low speed until the yolks are completely incorporated, scraping down the bowl occasionally with a rubber spatula. Slowly add the flour mixture and beat on low speed just until incorporated.

3 Put the pecans in a small bowl. Scoop up a rounded tablespoonful of the dough, then roll the dough between the palms of your hands into a ball. Lightly roll the dough ball in the pecans to coat it completely and place on the prepared cookie sheet. Repeat with the remaining dough, spacing the dough balls about 2 inches apart.

4 Using your thumb, press an indentation about ¼ inch deep in the center of each cookie. Carefully spoon about ½ teaspoon of the jam into each indentation. Bake until the cookie bottoms and edges are lightly browned, 20–25 minutes.

5 Let the cookies cool on the cookie sheet for 5 minutes, then, using a wide metal spatula, transfer to wire racks to cool completely, about 30 minutes. Store the cookies in an airtight container at room temperature for up to 3 days.

2 cups all-purpose flour

¼ teaspoon salt

1 cup unsalted butter, at room temperature

¾ cup granulated sugar

2 large egg yolks

2 teaspoons vanilla extract

1 cup finely chopped pecans

¼ cup blackberry jam

MAKES 20 COOKIES

CINNAMON-SUGAR SNICKERDOODLES

Dress up simple sugar cookies by rolling them in a cinnamon-sugar mixture just before baking. The grains of cinnamon and sugar add an appealing crunchy contrast to the soft interior of the cookies.

2¾ cups all-purpose flour

1 teaspoon baking powder

¼ teaspoon salt

1 cup unsalted butter, at room temperature

1¾ cups granulated sugar

2 large eggs

2 teaspoons vanilla extract

1 teaspoon ground cinnamon

MAKES 36 COOKIES

1 Position a rack in the middle of the oven and preheat to 350°F. Line 3 large cookie sheets with parchment paper.

2 In a bowl, sift together the flour, baking powder, and salt; set aside. In a large bowl, combine the butter and 1½ cups of the sugar. Using a mixer on medium speed, beat until well blended, about 1 minute. Add the eggs and vanilla and beat on low speed until the eggs are completely incorporated, scraping down the bowl occasionally with a rubber spatula. Slowly add the flour mixture and beat on low speed just until incorporated.

3 In a small bowl, stir together the remaining ¼ cup sugar and the cinnamon. Scoop up a rounded tablespoonful of the dough, then roll the dough between the palms of your hands into a ball. Lightly roll the dough ball in the cinnamon-sugar to coat it completely, and place on a prepared cookie sheet. Repeat with the remaining dough, spacing the dough balls about 3 inches apart. Bake, 1 sheet at a time, until the cookie edges are lightly browned but the tops are barely colored, 10–12 minutes.

4 Let the cookies cool on the cookie sheet for 5 minutes, then, using a wide metal spatula, transfer to wire racks to cool completely, about 30 minutes. Store the cookies in an airtight container at room temperature for up to 3 days.

CHOCOLATE, PISTACHIO & CHERRY BISCOTTI

This golden cookie provides a neutral background for green pistachios and red dried cherries, making these a perfect choice for a holiday cookie platter.

1 Position a rack in the middle of the oven and preheat to 350°F. Line 1 large cookie sheet with parchment paper.

2 In a bowl, sift together the flour, cocoa powder, baking powder, and salt; set aside. In a large bowl, combine the butter and sugar. Using a mixer on medium speed, beat until well blended, 1–2 minutes. Add the eggs and vanilla and almond extracts and beat on low speed until combined, then beat in the flour mixture just until incorporated. Add the pistachios and cherries and beat just until distributed.

3 Divide the dough in half. Spoon half of the dough onto the prepared cookie sheet to make a strip about 10 inches long, then press into a 10-by-2½-inch log. Repeat with the remaining dough half, leaving 4 inches of space between the 2 logs. Bake until the edges are light brown and the tops feel firm, 17–20 minutes. Let cool for about 10 minutes. Reduce the oven temperature to 325°F. Using a serrated knife, cut each log into 16 slices about ¾ inch wide. Place the slices, cut side down, on the cookie sheet and bake until the outsides are crisp and the edges turn dark golden, about 20 minutes.

4 Let the biscotti cool on the cookie sheet for 5 minutes, then transfer to wire racks to cool completely. Store in an airtight container at room temperature for up to 1 week.

1¾ cups all-purpose flour

¼ cup Dutch-process cocoa powder

1½ teaspoons baking powder

½ teaspoon salt

¾ cup unsalted butter, at room temperature

¾ cup granulated sugar

2 large eggs

1 teaspoon vanilla extract

½ teaspoon almond extract

1 cup coarsely chopped unsalted roasted pistachio nuts

¾ cup dried cherries

MAKES 32 COOKIES

DOUBLE-GINGER BISCOTTI

This recipe uses two types of ginger for maximum flavor. For the best taste, use ground ginger and cinnamon from recently opened jars. Look for crystallized ginger in specialty-food stores.

2 cups all-purpose flour

2 teaspoons ground ginger

1½ teaspoons baking powder

1 teaspoon ground cinnamon

½ teaspoon salt

¾ cup unsalted butter, at room temperature

¾ cup granulated sugar

2 large eggs

1 teaspoon vanilla extract

½ cup minced crystallized ginger

MAKES 32 COOKIES

1 Position a rack in the middle of the oven and preheat to 350°F. Line 1 large cookie sheet with parchment paper.

2 In a bowl, sift together the flour, ground ginger, baking powder, cinnamon, and salt; set aside. In a large bowl, combine the butter and sugar. Using a mixer on medium speed, beat until well blended, about 1 minute. Add the eggs and vanilla and beat on low speed until the eggs are completely incorporated, scraping down the bowl occasionally with a rubber spatula. Slowly add the flour mixture and beat on low speed just until incorporated. Add the crystallized ginger and beat just until distributed.

3 Divide the dough in half. Place large spoonfuls of the first half onto the prepared cookie sheet to make a strip about 10 inches long. Gently press the dough into a 10-by-2½-inch rectangular log. Repeat with the remaining dough half, leaving 4 inches of space between the 2 logs. Bake until the edges are light brown and the tops feel firm, 17–20 minutes. Let the logs stand on the cookie sheet for about 10 minutes. Reduce the oven temperature to 325°F. Using a serrated knife, cut each log into 16 slices about ¾ inch wide. Place the slices, cut side down, at least ¾ inch apart on the cookie sheet,

then bake until the outsides are crisp and the edges turn dark golden, about 20 minutes.

4 Let the biscotti cool on the cookie sheet for 5 minutes, then, using a metal spatula, transfer to wire racks to cool completely, about 30 minutes. Store the biscotti in an airtight container at room temperature for up to 1 week.

TOASTED HAZELNUT BISCOTTI

These Italian twice-baked cookies are perfect for dunking in coffee or wine.
If you like, substitute toasted almonds, pine nuts, or pecans for the hazelnuts.

1 Position a rack in the middle of the oven and preheat to 350°F.
Line 1 large cookie sheet with parchment paper.

2 In a bowl, sift together the flour, baking powder, and salt; set
aside. In a large bowl, combine the butter and sugar. Using a
mixer on medium speed, beat until well blended, about 1 minute. Add
the eggs and vanilla and beat on low speed until incorporated. Slowly
add the flour mixture and beat on low speed just until incorporated.
Add the toasted hazelnuts and beat just until distributed.

3 Divide the dough in half. Place large spoonfuls of the first half
onto the prepared cookie sheet to make a strip about 10 inches
long. Gently press the dough into a 10-by-2½-inch rectangular log.
Repeat with the remaining dough half, leaving 4 inches of space
between the 2 logs. Bake until the edges are light brown and the
tops feel firm, 17–20 minutes. Let the logs stand on the cookie sheet
for about 10 minutes. Reduce the oven temperature to 325°F. Using
a serrated knife, cut each log into 16 slices about ¾ inch wide. Place
the slices, cut side down, at least ¾ inch apart on the cookie sheet,
then bake until the outsides are crisp and the edges turn dark golden,
about 20 minutes.

4 Let the biscotti cool on the cookie sheet for 5 minutes, then
transfer to wire racks to cool completely, about 30 minutes.
Store in an airtight container at room temperature for up to 1 week.

2 cups all-purpose flour

1½ teaspoons baking
powder

½ teaspoon salt

¾ cup unsalted butter,
at room temperature

¾ cup granulated sugar

2 large eggs

1 teaspoon vanilla extract

1 cup finely chopped
toasted and skinned
hazelnuts

MAKES 32 COOKIES

PIPED
COOKIES

Piped cookies rely on a
specialized cookie press or
canvas pastry bag to create their
unique forms—from floral shapes
and delicate kisses to a ridged
whipped cream cookie filling.

BUTTER SPRITZ COOKIES

This versatile dough, extruded through a traditional cookie press into fanciful shapes, can be made more decorative by adding a few drops of food coloring or two teaspoons finely grated citrus zest.

1 cup unsalted butter, at room temperature

⅔ cup granulated sugar

¼ teaspoon salt

2 large egg yolks

2 teaspoons vanilla extract

2¼ cups all-purpose flour

sugar crystals for sprinkling, optional

MAKES 80 COOKIES

1 Position a rack in the middle of the oven and preheat to 350°F. Have ready 3 large cookie sheets.

2 In a large bowl, combine the butter, granulated sugar, and salt. Using a mixer on medium speed, beat until well blended, about 1 minute. Add the egg yolks and vanilla and beat on low speed until the yolks are completely incorporated. Slowly add the flour and beat on low speed just until incorporated.

3 With lightly floured hands, form one-third of the dough into a log that fits into the cookie press cylinder. Pack the dough firmly into the cookie press, using a small spoon, if necessary. Following the manufacturer's instructions, fit the cylinder with the disk of your choice. Hold the press upright and position it over a cookie sheet so it's touching lightly, then press the dough out onto the sheet. Lift the press away as soon as each cookie is formed, spacing them 1 inch apart. Sprinkle the cookies lightly with sugar crystals, if desired. Bake, 1 sheet at a time, until the cookie bottoms and edges are lightly browned, 12–15 minutes.

4 Let the cookies cool on the cookie sheet for 5 minutes, then, using a wide metal spatula, transfer to wire racks to cool completely, about 30 minutes. Repeat to form and bake the remaining cookies. Store in an airtight container at room temperature for up to 3 days.

CHOCOLATE MACAROONS

Serve these delicious cookies plain, or sandwiched with Chocolate Filling (page 106) following the instructions for Almond-Filled Macaroons (page 56).

1 Position a rack in the middle of the oven and preheat to 400 °F. Line 2 large cookie sheets with parchment paper. Have ready 2 additional cookie sheets.

2 In a food processor, combine the almonds, confectioners' sugar, and cocoa powder. Pulse briefly, then process until finely ground, about 2 minutes. Transfer to a large bowl. In a clean bowl, combine the egg whites and cream of tartar. Using a mixer on medium speed, beat until foamy, about 1 minute, then beat on medium-high speed until soft peaks form, 2–3 minutes. Slowly add the superfine sugar and beat until stiff peaks form, about 1 minute longer. Beat in the almond extract. Using a rubber spatula, in 2 batches, gently fold the egg whites into the almond mixture until no white streaks remain.

3 Spoon the dough into a large pastry bag fitted with a ½-inch plain pastry tip. Pipe the dough onto the prepared cookie sheets in 1-inch circles spaced 1 inch apart. Let stand, uncovered, for 1 hour.

4 Stack each sheet of cookies on an empty sheet. Put 1 batch in the oven and reduce the heat to 350 °F. Bake until the tops are lightly golden, 8–10 minutes. Let stand for 3 minutes, then gently transfer to wire racks to cool completely, about 30 minutes. Return the oven to 400°F and repeat with the second batch. Store the cookies in an airtight container at room temperature for up to 3 days.

1 cup blanched almonds

2½ cups confectioners' sugar

¼ cup Dutch-process cocoa powder

4 large egg whites

¼ teaspoon cream of tartar

¼ cup superfine sugar

½ teaspoon almond extract

MAKES 28 COOKIES

ALMOND-FILLED MACAROONS

Though fancy looking, these nutty macaroons, popular in Parisian pastry shops, are surprisingly easy to make. To ensure the correct texture, be sure to let them dry for an hour before baking.

1 cup blanched almonds

2 cups confectioners' sugar

4 large egg whites

¼ teaspoon cream of tartar

¼ cup superfine sugar

½ teaspoon almond extract

Almond Filling, page 106

MAKES 30 COOKIES

1 Position a rack in the middle of the oven and preheat to 400°F. Line 2 large cookie sheets with parchment paper. Have ready 2 additional cookie sheets.

2 In a food processor, combine the almonds and confectioners' sugar. Pulse briefly, then process until finely ground, about 2 minutes. Transfer to a large bowl. In a clean bowl, combine the egg whites and cream of tartar. Using a mixer on medium speed, beat until foamy, about 1 minute. Increase the speed to medium-high and beat until the egg whites look shiny and soft peaks form, 2–3 minutes. Slowly add the superfine sugar and beat until stiff peaks form, about 1 minute longer. Beat in the almond extract. Using a rubber spatula, in 2 batches, gently fold the egg whites into the almond mixture until no white streaks remain.

3 Spoon the dough into a large pastry bag fitted with a ½-inch plain pastry tip. Pipe the dough onto the parchment-lined cookie sheets in 1-inch circles spaced 1 inch apart. Let stand at room temperature, uncovered, for 1 hour. Stack each sheet of cookies on an empty sheet. Put 1 batch in the oven and reduce the heat to 350°F. Bake until the tops are lightly golden, 8–10 minutes. Let stand for 3 minutes, then

gently transfer to wire racks to cool completely, about 30 minutes. Return the oven to 400°F and repeat with the second batch.

4 Turn half of the cooled cookies bottom side up. Using an icing spatula, spread 1 teaspoon of the filling over each cookie bottom. Gently press the remaining cookies, bottom side down, onto the filling. Store the cookies in an airtight container at room temperature for up to 3 days.

PISTACHIO MACAROONS

The pistachios impart their distinctive flavor and color to these light, crisp French-style macaroons. To sandwich them with Almond Filling (page 106), follow the instructions for Almond-Filled Macaroons (page 56).

1 Position a rack in the middle of the oven and preheat to 400°F. Line 2 large cookie sheets with parchment paper. Have ready 2 additional cookie sheets.

2 In a food processor, combine the nuts and confectioners' sugar. Pulse briefly, then process until finely ground, about 2 minutes. Transfer to a large bowl. In a clean bowl, combine the egg whites and cream of tartar. Using a mixer on medium speed, beat until foamy, about 1 minute, then beat on medium-high speed until soft peaks form, 2–3 minutes. Slowly add the superfine sugar and beat until stiff peaks form, about 1 minute longer. Beat in the almond extract. Using a rubber spatula, in 2 batches, gently fold the egg whites into the pistachio mixture until no white streaks remain.

3 Spoon the dough into a large pastry bag fitted with a ½-inch plain pastry tip. Pipe the dough onto the prepared cookie sheets in 1-inch circles spaced 1 inch apart. Let stand, uncovered, for 1 hour.

4 Stack each sheet of cookies on an empty sheet. Put 1 batch in the oven and reduce the heat to 350°F. Bake until the tops are lightly golden, 8–10 minutes. Let stand for 3 minutes, then gently transfer to wire racks to cool completely, about 30 minutes. Return the oven to 400°F and repeat with the second batch. Store the cookies in an airtight container at room temperature for up to 3 days.

1 cup shelled unsalted roasted pistachio nuts

2 cups confectioners' sugar

4 large egg whites

¼ teaspoon cream of tartar

¼ cup superfine sugar

½ teaspoon almond extract

MAKES 30 COOKIES

CREAM-FILLED PECAN LACE COOKIES

These crisp, candylike cookies are formed into decorative tubes then filled with lightly sweetened whipped cream. For optimum crispness, make them on a day that is not humid or rainy.

4 tablespoons unsalted butter, cut into 4 equal pieces

⅓ cup granulated sugar

2 tablespoons light corn syrup

⅓ cup all-purpose flour

1 cup finely chopped pecans

1 teaspoon vanilla extract

Sweetened Whipped Cream, page 107

MAKES 27 COOKIES

1 Position a rack in the middle of the oven and preheat to 350°F. Line 3 large cookie sheets with parchment paper or nonstick silicone liners.

2 In a heavy saucepan over low heat, combine the butter, sugar, and corn syrup. Heat, stirring often with a wooden spoon, until the butter melts and the sugar dissolves. Raise the heat to medium-high and bring to a boil while stirring constantly. Remove the pan from the heat and stir in the flour until it is incorporated. Stir in the pecans and vanilla.

3 Scoop up a rounded tablespoonful of dough and place it on a prepared cookie sheet. Repeat with the remaining dough, spacing the dough drops about 3 inches apart. Bake, 1 sheet at a time, until the cookie bottoms and edges are lightly browned but the tops are lightly golden in the center, 8–10 minutes.

4 As soon as the cookies come out of the oven, use an icing spatula to lift each cookie off the baking sheet and mold it around a 2-inch dowel. Let stand until set, about 10 minutes, then gently slide

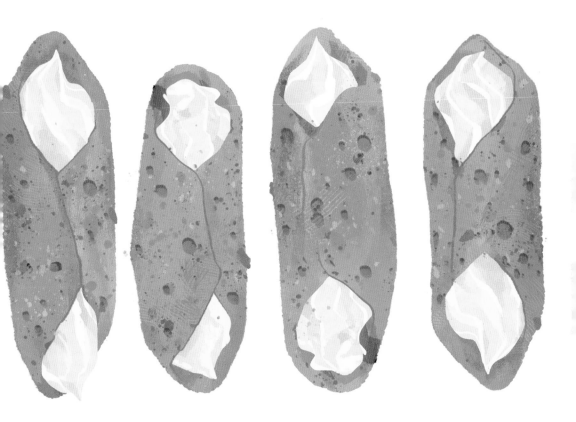

the cookies off the dowel. Transfer the cookies to wire racks to cool completely, about 30 minutes. Repeat to bake and cool the remaining cookies. Store the unfilled cookies in an airtight container at room temperature for up to 2 days.

5 To fill the cookies, spoon the whipped cream into a large pastry bag fitted with a ½-inch star tip. Squeeze the cream into the centers of the cookies, filling them evenly. Serve right away.

ROLLED AND CUT COOKIES

These cookies showcase easy-to-roll doughs in a variety of interesting forms: shapes cut with cookie cutters; pinwheels spun from rolled and chilled dough logs; and classic crescents stuffed with sweet fillings.

SUGAR COOKIE CUTOUTS

Use cookie cutters to make cookies in a variety of fanciful shapes. The key is a sturdy, easy-to-roll dough that holds its shape during baking.

1 In a bowl, sift together the 2½ cups flour, the baking powder, and salt; set aside. In a large bowl, combine the butter and granulated sugar. Using a mixer on medium speed, beat until well blended, about 1 minute. Add the egg and vanilla and almond extracts and beat on low speed until blended. Beat in the flour mixture just until incorporated. Divide the dough in half and press each piece into a 6-inch disk. Wrap each disk tightly in plastic wrap and refrigerate until firm, at least 1 hour or up to overnight.

2 Position a rack in the middle of the oven and preheat to 350°F. Line 3 large cookie sheets with parchment paper.

3 Place 1 chilled dough disk on a floured work surface. Using a floured rolling pin, roll out the disk to about ¼ inch thick. Using a cookie cutter, cut out as many cookies as possible. Use a metal spatula to transfer the cookies to the prepared sheets, spacing them 1 inch apart. Press the dough scraps into a ball and refrigerate until firm. Repeat with the remaining chilled dough disk and scraps.

4 Bake, 1 sheet at a time, until the cookie bottoms and edges are lightly browned but the tops are barely colored, 10–13 minutes. Let cool on the cookie sheet for 5 minutes, then, transfer to wire racks to cool completely, about 30 minutes. Pipe or drizzle the glaze over the cookies, then sprinkle the glaze with the crystals, if desired. Store in an airtight container at room temperature for up to 3 days.

2½ cups all-purpose flour, plus extra for dusting

½ teaspoon baking powder

¼ teaspoon salt

1 cup unsalted butter, at room temperature

1 cup granulated sugar

1 large egg

2 teaspoons vanilla extract

½ teaspoon almond extract

Vanilla Glaze, page 104, optional

sugar crystals for sprinkling, optional

MAKES 40 COOKIES

ZESTY LIME SUGAR COOKIES

Finely grated lime zest adds a burst of citrus flavor to these cookies. If you plan to glaze them, consider adding a drop of green food coloring to the glaze to hint at the cookies' lime flavor.

2½ cups all-purpose flour, plus extra for dusting

½ teaspoon baking powder

½ teaspoon ground cinnamon

¼ teaspoon salt

1 cup unsalted butter, at room temperature

1 cup granulated sugar

1 large egg

1 tablespoon finely grated lime zest

2 teaspoons vanilla extract

½ teaspoon almond extract

Vanilla Glaze, page 104, optional

sugar crystals for sprinkling, optional

MAKES 40 COOKIES

1 In a bowl, sift together the 2½ cups flour, the baking powder, cinnamon, and salt; set aside. In a large bowl, combine the butter and granulated sugar. Using a mixer on medium speed, beat until well blended, about 1 minute. Add the egg, zest, and vanilla and almond extracts and beat on low speed until the eggs are incorporated, scraping down the bowl occasionally with a rubber spatula. Slowly add the flour mixture and beat on low speed just until incorporated. Divide the dough in half and press each piece into a 6-inch disk. Wrap each disk tightly in plastic wrap and refrigerate until firm, at least 1 hour or up to overnight.

2 Position a rack in the middle of the oven and preheat to 350°F. Line 3 large cookie sheets with parchment paper.

3 Place 1 chilled dough disk on a floured work surface. Using a floured rolling pin, roll out the disk to about ¼ inch thick. Using a cookie cutter, cut out as many cookies as possible. Use a metal spatula to transfer the cookies to the prepared sheets, spacing them 1 inch apart. Press the dough scraps into a ball and refrigerate until firm. Repeat with the remaining chilled dough disk and scraps.

4 Bake, 1 sheet at a time, until the cookie bottoms and edges are lightly browned but the tops are barely colored, 10–13 minutes.

Let cool on the cookie sheet for 5 minutes, then, using the metal spatula, transfer to wire racks to cool completely, about 30 minutes. Pipe or drizzle the glaze over the cookies, then sprinkle the glaze with the crystals, if desired. Store the cookies in an airtight container at room temperature for up to 3 days.

BLACK-AND-WHITE COOKIES

Dark chocolate and snow-white glazes contrast beautifully on these stunning cookies. Change the color scheme by adding a few drops of food coloring to the white glaze, if you like.

1 Follow the recipe to make and roll out the dough for the Sugar Cookie Cutouts, then cut the dough into rounds using a 3-inch round cookie cutter. Bake and cool the cookies as directed.

2 While the cookies are cooling, make the chocolate glaze: In a large metal bowl that fits on the rim of a saucepan, combine the cream, butter, corn syrup, and chocolate. Place the bowl on the saucepan over, but not touching, barely simmering water. Heat, stirring constantly, until the chocolate is melted and smooth, 3–4 minutes. Set aside to cool and thicken, about 45 minutes at room temperature or 15 minutes if covered and refrigerated.

3 Meanwhile, make the glaze: Sift the confectioners' sugar into a bowl. Add the hot water, corn syrup, and almond extract and stir until smooth.

4 Spoon a teaspoon of the white glaze on 1 side of each cookie. Use the back of a spoon to spread the glaze over half of the cookie. (If the glaze becomes too thick to spread, stir in a few drops of hot water.) Next, spoon 1 teaspoon of the chocolate glaze over the unglazed half of each cookie, spreading it evenly. Transfer the cookies to a waxed paper—lined cookie sheet and refrigerate until the glaze is firm, about 30 minutes, or cover with plastic wrap and refrigerate for up to 3 days. Bring the cookies to room temperature before serving.

Sugar Cookie Cutouts, page 65

FOR CHOCOLATE GLAZE

¼ cup heavy whipping cream

¼ cup unsalted butter, cut into ½-inch pieces

3 tablespoons light corn syrup

5 ounces semisweet chocolate, chopped

FOR SNOW-WHITE GLAZE

3 cups confectioners' sugar

4 tablespoons hot water

2 tablespoons corn syrup

½ teaspoon almond extract

MAKES 40 COOKIES

CHOCOLATE-ORANGE STRIPE COOKIES

Striped cookies are easy to make. Simply line small loaf pans with aluminum foil, pack the dough into the pans, then lift the foil to remove the dough, and slice and bake the cookies as directed.

2 cups all-purpose flour

½ teaspoon baking powder

¼ teaspoon salt

1 cup unsalted butter, at room temperature

1 cup granulated sugar

2 large eggs, separated

2 teaspoons vanilla extract

2 teaspoons grated orange zest

2 tablespoons Dutch-process cocoa powder

MAKES 40 COOKIES

1 Line each of two 5-by-3½-by-2 inch loaf pans with a 10-inch piece of aluminum foil. Press the foil into the bottom and over the sides of the pans.

2 In a bowl, sift together the flour, baking powder, and salt; set aside. In a large bowl, combine the butter and sugar. Using a mixer on medium speed, beat until well blended, about 1 minute. Add the egg yolks and vanilla and beat on low speed until the yolks are completely incorporated, scraping down the bowl occasionally. Slowly add the flour mixture and beat just until incorporated. Remove half of the dough from the bowl. Add the zest to the dough in the bowl, beat on low speed until incorporated, then remove the dough. Place the vanilla dough in the bowl, sift in the cocoa powder, then beat until the dough is evenly colored. Cut both dough halves into 4 equal pieces. Spread 1 piece of orange dough evenly in a lined pan. Spread 1 piece of chocolate dough over the orange dough. Repeat with another piece of orange and then chocolate dough. Repeat with the remaining dough and second pan. Cover both pans with plastic wrap and refrigerate for at least 2 hours.

3 Position a rack in the middle of the oven and preheat to 325°F. Line 3 large cookie sheets with parchment paper. Holding the foil, lift the dough onto a cutting surface. Cut the dough into ¼-inch slices and place them 2 inches apart on the sheets. Bake, 1 sheet at a time, until the tops feel firm and the bottoms are light golden, 11–13 minutes. Let cool on the cookie sheet for 5 minutes, then transfer to wire racks to cool completely, about 30 minutes. Store the cookies in an airtight container at room temperature for up to 5 days.

CHOCOLATE SPICE COOKIES

These spicy treats are infused with cinnamon, nutmeg, and allspice. To embellish them, use the glazes for Black-and-White Cookies (page 69) or dust them lightly with confectioners' sugar.

1 In a bowl, sift together the 2½ cups flour, the cocoa powder, cinnamon, nutmeg, baking soda, salt, and allspice; set aside. In a large bowl, combine the butter and sugar. Using a mixer on medium speed, beat until well blended, about 1 minute. Add the egg and vanilla and almond extracts and beat until the egg is incorporated, scraping down the bowl occasionally with a rubber spatula. Slowly add the flour mixture and beat on low speed just until incorporated. Divide the dough in half and press each piece into a 6-inch disk. Wrap each disk tightly in plastic wrap and refrigerate until firm, at least 1 hour or up to overnight.

2 Position a rack in the middle of the oven and preheat to 350°F. Line 3 large cookie sheets with parchment paper.

3 Place 1 chilled dough disk on a floured work surface. Using a floured rolling pin, roll out the disk to about ¼ inch thick. Using a cookie cutter, cut out as many cookies as possible. Use a metal spatula to transfer the cookies to the prepared sheets, spacing them 1 inch apart. Press the dough scraps into a ball and refrigerate until firm. Repeat with the remaining chilled dough disk and scraps.

4 Bake, 1 sheet at a time, until just the edges are lightly browned, 10–13 minutes. Let cool on the cookie sheet for 5 minutes, then, using the metal spatula, transfer to wire racks to cool completely. Store in an airtight container at room temperature for up to 3 days.

2½ cups all-purpose flour, plus extra for dusting

2 tablespoons Dutch-process cocoa powder

1 teaspoon ground cinnamon

½ teaspoon freshly grated nutmeg

½ teaspoon baking soda

¼ teaspoon salt

¼ teaspoon ground allspice

1 cup unsalted butter, at room temperature

1 cup granulated sugar

1 large egg

2 teaspoons vanilla extract

½ teaspoon almond extract

MAKES 40 COOKIES

PINWHEEL ICEBOX COOKIES

Making these eye-catching, swirl-patterned cookies is simple: make a vanilla dough, add cocoa powder to half of it, then roll the halves together. Chill the roll, then slice and bake the cookies.

2 cups all-purpose flour

½ teaspoon baking powder

¼ teaspoon salt

1 cup unsalted butter, at room temperature

1 cup granulated sugar

2 large eggs, separated

2 teaspoons vanilla extract

2 tablespoons Dutch-process cocoa powder

MAKES 54 COOKIES

1 In a bowl, sift together the flour, baking powder, and salt; set aside. In a large bowl, combine the butter and sugar. Using a mixer on medium speed, beat until well blended, about 1 minute. Add the egg yolks and vanilla and beat on low speed until the yolks are completely incorporated, scraping down the bowl occasionally. Slowly add the flour mixture and beat just until incorporated. Form half of the dough into a 6-inch disk and set aside. Sift the cocoa over the remaining dough, beat until the dough is evenly colored, then form it into a 6-inch disk. Wrap both disks in plastic wrap and refrigerate for about 30 minutes.

2 Whisk the egg whites until foamy. Roll out each dough disk between 2 sheets of waxed paper to about 14 by 8 inches. Slowly remove the top sheets of paper. Brush the cocoa dough with the egg white and place the vanilla dough, paper side up, directly on top of the chocolate dough. Slowly remove the top sheet of paper. Starting at the long side, roll the dough layers into a tight cylinder, peeling off the bottom sheet of paper as you go. Seal the seam, trim the ends evenly, wrap the log tightly with waxed paper, and refrigerate until firm, at least 2 hours.

3 Position a rack in the middle of the oven and preheat to 325°F. Line 3 large cookie sheets with parchment paper. Cut the log into ¼ inch slices and place them 1 inch apart on the sheets. Bake, 1 sheet at a time, until the tops feel firm and the bottoms are golden, 11–13 minutes. Let cool on the cookie sheet for 5 minutes, then, using a wide metal spatula, transfer to wire racks to cool completely, about 30 minutes. Store the cookies in an airtight container at room temperature for up to 5 days.

RASPBERRY PINWHEELS

To make the purée for these whimsical pink-and-white swirled cookies, whirl one cup fresh or unsweetened frozen raspberries in a food processor until smooth and strain to remove the seeds.

2 cups plus 5 tablespoons all-purpose flour

½ teaspoon baking powder

¼ teaspoon salt

1 cup unsalted butter, at room temperature

1 cup granulated sugar

2 separated large eggs

2 teaspoons vanilla extract

3 tablespoons (see note) raspberry purée

MAKES 54 COOKIES

1 In a bowl, sift together the 2 cups flour, the baking powder, and the salt; set aside. In a bowl, combine the butter and sugar. Using a mixer on medium speed, beat until well blended, about 1 minute. Add the egg yolks and vanilla and beat on low speed until the yolks are completely incorporated, scraping down the bowl occasionally. Slowly add the flour mixture and beat just until incorporated. Form half of the dough into a 6-inch disk; set aside. Add the raspberry purée and the 5 tablespoons flour to the remaining dough, beat until evenly colored, then form it into a 6-inch disk. Wrap both disks in plastic wrap and refrigerate for about 30 minutes.

2 Whisk the egg whites until foamy. Roll out each dough disk between 2 sheets of waxed paper to about 14 by 8 inches. Slowly remove the top sheets of paper. Brush the raspberry dough with the egg white and place the vanilla dough, paper side up, directly on top of the raspberry dough. Slowly remove the top sheet of paper. Starting at the long side, roll the dough layers into a tight cylinder, peeling off the bottom sheet of paper as you go. Seal the seam, trim the ends evenly, wrap the log tightly with waxed paper, and refrigerate until firm, at least 2 hours.

3 Position a rack in the middle of the oven and preheat to 325°F. Line 3 large cookie sheets with parchment paper. Cut the log into ¼ inch slices and place them 1 inch apart on the sheets. Bake, 1 sheet at a time, until the tops feel firm and the bottoms are golden, 11–13 minutes. Let cool on the cookie sheet for 5 minutes, then transfer to wire racks to cool completely, about 30 minutes. Store the cookies in an airtight container at room temperature for up to 5 days.

APRICOT RUGELACH

Here, a traditional Eastern European cream cheese dough encloses jam and dried fruit in golden, bite-size crescents.

1 In a large bowl, stir together the 2¼ cups flour, the sugar, and salt. Add the cream cheese and, using a mixer on low speed, beat until until blended, about 30 seconds. Add the butter and beat until large clumps of dough form, about 1 minute. Add the sour cream and vanilla and beat until well blended. Cut the dough into 4 equal pieces and form each into a 3-inch disk. Wrap each disk tightly in plastic wrap and refrigerate until firm, at least 45 minutes.

2 Position a rack in the middle of the oven and preheat to 375°F. Line 2 large cookie sheets with parchment paper.

3 One at a time, remove the dough disks from the refrigerator and place on a floured work surface. Using a floured rolling pin, roll out each disk into a 10-inch circle. Spread 2 tablespoons of the apricot preserves over each dough circle, leaving a ¾-inch border on the edges and a 1-inch circle in the center uncovered. Sprinkle one-fourth of the apricot pieces over each circle.

4 Cut each round into 12 wedges. Beginning at a wide end, roll up each wedge to form a tight cylinder. Place the cylinders 1 inch apart on a cookie sheet with the tip facing down. Bend the ends to form a slight crescent. Bake, 1 sheet at a time, until golden, 15–18 minutes. Let cool on the sheet for 5 minutes. Transfer to wire racks to cool for 10 minutes more. Brush the still-warm tops with the glaze. Store in an airtight container at room temperature for up to 3 days.

2¼ cups all-purpose flour, plus extra for dusting

¼ cup granulated sugar

¼ teaspoon salt

6 ounces cream cheese, at room temperature

1¼ cups cold unsalted butter, cut into ½-inch pieces

2 tablespoons sour cream

2 teaspoons vanilla extract

½ cup apricot preserves

½ cup chopped dried apricots (¼–½-inch pieces)

Vanilla Glaze, page 104

MAKES 48 COOKIES

MEDJOOL DATE RUGELACH

Medjool dates are large, especially soft dried fruits that are prized for their tender skin and creamy texture. Because of their size, the filling for these cookies requires only about four dates.

2¼ cups all-purpose flour, plus extra for dusting

¼ cup granulated sugar

¼ teaspoon salt

6 ounces cream cheese, at room temperature

1¼ cups cold unsalted butter, cut into ½-inch pieces, plus ¼ cup

2 tablespoons sour cream

2 teaspoons vanilla extract

1 teaspoon ground cinnamon

½ cup chopped (¼–½-inch pieces) Medjool dates

Vanilla Glaze, page 104

MAKES 48 COOKIES

1 In a large bowl, stir together the flour, sugar, and salt. Add the cream cheese and, using a mixer on low speed, beat until the ingredients are blended, about 30 seconds. Add the butter pieces and beat until large clumps of dough form, about 1 minute. Add the sour cream and vanilla and beat until well blended. Cut the dough into 4 equal pieces and form each into a 3-inch disk. Wrap each disk tightly in plastic wrap and refrigerate until firm, at least 45 minutes.

2 Position a rack in the middle of the oven and preheat to 375°F. Line 2 large cookie sheets with parchment paper.

3 In a small saucepan, melt the ¼ cup butter with the cinnamon; set aside. One at a time, remove the dough disks from the refrigerator and place on a floured work surface. Using a floured rolling pin, roll out each disk into a 10-inch circle. Brush the cinnamon butter over each dough circle, leaving a ¾-inch border on the edges and a 1-inch circle in the center uncovered. Sprinkle one-fourth of the date pieces over each dough circle.

4 Cut each round into 12 wedges. Beginning at the wide ends, roll the edge over the filling to form a tight cylinder; do not squeeze out the filling. Place the cylinders 1 inch apart on a cookie sheet with

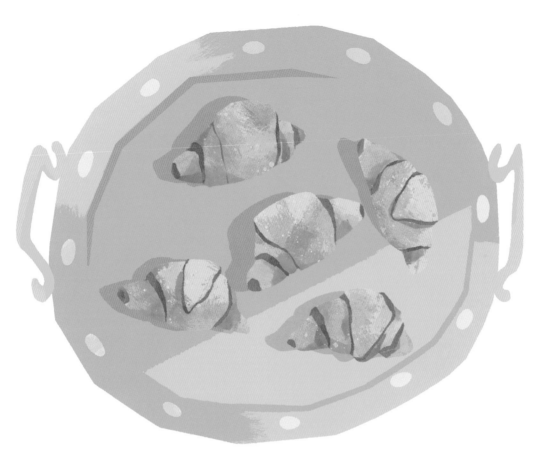

the tip facing down. Bend the ends to form a slight crescent. Bake,
1 sheet at a time, until the edges are golden, 15–18 minutes. Let cool
on the sheet for 5 minutes, then transfer to wire racks to cool for about
10 minutes. Brush the still-warm tops lightly with the glaze. Store in
an airtight container at room temperature for up to 3 days.

CHOCOLATE CHIP RUGELACH

Using miniature chocolate chips instead of regular ones makes these cookies easier to roll. The apricot preserves add a slightly tangy taste.

1 In a large bowl, stir together the 2¼ cups flour, the sugar, and salt. Add the cream cheese and, using a mixer on low speed, beat until the ingredients are blended, about 30 seconds. Add the butter and beat until large clumps of dough form, about 1 minute. Add the sour cream and vanilla and beat until well blended. Cut the dough into 4 equal pieces and form each into a 3-inch disk. Wrap each disk tightly in plastic wrap and refrigerate until firm, at least 45 minutes.

2 Position a rack in the middle of the oven and preheat to 375°F. Line 2 large cookie sheets with parchment paper.

3 One at a time, remove the dough disks from the refrigerator and place on a floured work surface. Using a floured rolling pin, roll out each disk into a 10-inch circle. Spread 1 tablespoon of the apricot preserves over each dough circle, leaving a ¾-inch border on the edges and a 1-inch circle in the center uncovered. Sprinkle one-fourth of the chocolate chips over each dough circle.

4 Cut each round into 12 wedges. Beginning at the wide ends, roll the edge over the filling to form a cylinder. Place the cylinders 1 inch apart on a cookie sheet with the tip facing down. Bend the ends to form a crescent. Bake, 1 sheet at a time, until the edges are golden, 15–18 minutes. Let cool on the sheet for 5 minutes, then transfer to wire racks to cool for 10 minutes. Brush the warm tops with the glaze. Store in an airtight container at room temperature for up to 3 days.

2¼ cups all-purpose flour, plus extra for dusting

¼ cup granulated sugar

¼ teaspoon salt

6 ounces cream cheese, at room temperature

1¼ cups cold unsalted butter, cut into ½-inch pieces

2 tablespoons sour cream

2 teaspoons vanilla extract

¼ cup apricot preserves

1 cup miniature semisweet chocolate chips

Vanilla Glaze, page 104

MAKES 48 COOKIES

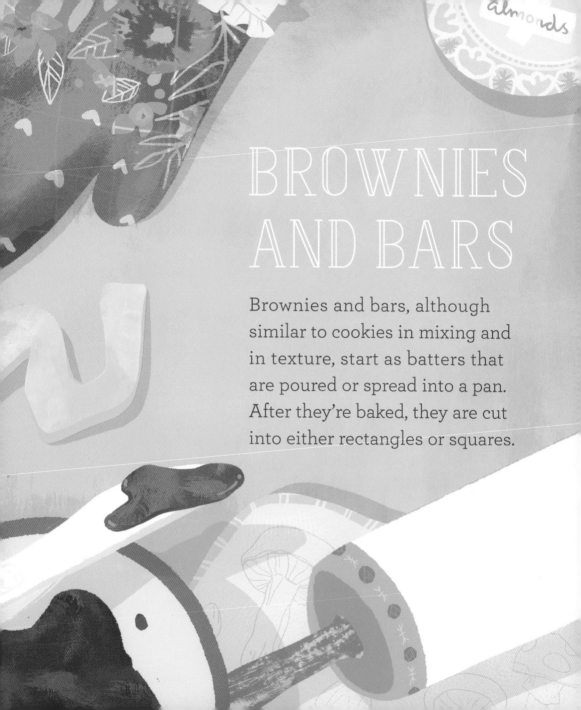

BROWNIES AND BARS

Brownies and bars, although similar to cookies in mixing and in texture, start as batters that are poured or spread into a pan. After they're baked, they are cut into either rectangles or squares.

COCONUT-LEMON SQUARES

Shreds of coconut add a chewy texture and tropical infusion to classic lemon bars. Be sure to use sweetened coconut for the best flavor.

1 Position a rack in the middle of the oven and preheat to 325°F. Press a 20-inch piece of aluminum foil onto the bottom and over the sides of a 13-by-9-by-2-inch baking pan. Butter the foil.

2 To make the crust, in a large bowl, combine the flour, confectioners' sugar, zest, and salt. Using a mixer on low speed, beat just until blended, about 1 minute. Add the butter and beat until the largest pieces are about the size of peas, about 2 minutes. Press the dough over the bottom and 1 inch up the sides of the prepared pan. Bake just until the edges are lightly browned, about 20 minutes. Remove from the oven and set aside. Reduce the oven temperature to 300°F.

3 To make the filling, in a large bowl, whisk the eggs just until blended. Add the granulated sugar and lemon juice and zest and whisk until smooth, about 1 minute. Add the coconut and mix well. Sift the flour into the bowl and whisk until incorporated. Slowly pour the filling over the crust. Bake until the filling looks set and does not wobble when the pan is shaken, 40–45 minutes. Transfer the pan to a wire rack and let cool until the top is room temperature, about 1 hour. Cover the pan with plastic wrap and refrigerate for at least 4 hours to firm.

4 Holding the ends of the foil, lift the bar onto a cutting surface. Using a large, sharp knife, cut the bar into 48 pieces. Store the squares in an airtight container in the refrigerator for up to 2 days.

FOR THE CRUST

1½ cups all-purpose flour

½ cup confectioners' sugar

1½ teaspoons finely grated lemon zest

⅛ teaspoon salt

¾ cup cold unsalted butter, cut into ½-inch pieces

FOR THE FILLING

6 large eggs

2½ cups granulated sugar

¾ cup fresh lemon juice

1 tablespoon finely grated lemon zest

2 cups sweetened shredded coconut

½ cup all-purpose flour

MAKES 48 SQUARES

RASPBERRY-ALMOND LINZER BARS

With bright red raspberry jam peeking through the rich almond lattice top, these versatile and easy-to-make bars are a beautiful choice for a holiday cookie platter or for filling a gift tin.

1 cup blanched almonds

1¾ cups all-purpose flour

½ cup granulated sugar

½ teaspoon baking powder

½ teaspoon ground cinnamon

¼ teaspoon salt

1 cup cold unsalted butter, cut into ½-inch pieces

1 large egg

1 teaspoon vanilla extract

½ teaspoon almond extract

1¼ cups seedless raspberry jam

MAKES 25 BARS

1 Position a rack in the middle of the oven and preheat to 325°F. Press a 15-inch piece of aluminum foil onto the bottom and over the sides of a 9-by-9-by-2-inch baking pan. Butter the foil.

2 In a food processor, pulse the almonds to chop coarsely, then process until finely ground, about 30 seconds. In a large bowl, combine the almonds, flour, sugar, baking powder, cinnamon, and salt. Using a mixer on low speed, beat just to blend the ingredients, about 1 minute. Add the butter and beat until the largest pieces are about the size of peas, about 1 minute. In a small bowl, whisk together the egg and vanilla and almond extracts. Add the egg mixture to the large bowl and beat until the dough pulls away from the sides, about 15 seconds.

3 Form 1 cup of the dough into a disk, wrap in plastic wrap, and refrigerate. Press the remaining dough over the bottom and 1 inch up the sides of the prepared pan. Spread the jam over the dough. Cut the chilled dough into 10 equal pieces. On a floured work surface with floured hands, roll each piece to make ten 9-by-½-inch ropes. Lay 5 ropes, 1 inch apart, over the jam. Then lay the remaining 5 ropes over

the first at an angle, 1 inch apart, to form a lattice pattern. Bake just
until the lattice is lightly browned, 35–40 minutes. Transfer to a wire
rack and let cool until room temperature, about 1 hour.

4 Holding the ends of the foil, lift the bar onto a cutting surface.
Using a large, sharp knife, cut the bar into 25 pieces. Store the
bars in an airtight container at room temperature for up to 3 days.

TANGY LEMON BARS

These lemon bars are a model of baking simplicity. The no-roll, butter-crumb crust is pressed directly into the pan and the pleasingly tart, silky-smooth filling requires very little mixing.

FOR THE CRUST

1½ cups all-purpose flour

½ cup confectioners' sugar

1½ teaspoons finely grated lemon zest

⅛ teaspoon salt

¾ cup cold unsalted butter, cut into ½-inch pieces

FOR THE FILLING

6 large eggs

2½ cups granulated sugar

¾ cup fresh lemon juice

1 tablespoon finely grated lemon zest

½ cup all-purpose flour

2 tablespoons confectioners' sugar, for dusting

MAKES 48 BARS

1 Position a rack in the middle of the oven and preheat to 325°F. Press a 20-inch piece of aluminum foil onto the bottom and over the sides of a 13-by-9-by-2-inch baking pan. Butter the foil.

2 To make the crust, in a large bowl, combine the flour, confectioners' sugar, zest, and salt. Using a mixer on low speed, beat just until blended, about 1 minute. Add the butter and beat until the largest pieces are the size of peas, 1–2 minutes. Press the dough over the bottom and 1 inch up the sides of the prepared pan. Bake just until the edges are lightly browned, about 20 minutes. Remove from the oven and set aside. Reduce the temperature to 300°F.

3 To make the filling, in a large bowl, whisk the eggs just until blended. Add the granulated sugar and lemon juice and zest and whisk until smooth, about 1 minute. Sift the flour into the bowl and whisk until incorporated. Slowly pour the filling over the crust. Bake until the filling looks set and does not wobble when the pan is shaken, 40–45 minutes. Transfer the pan to a wire rack and let cool. Cover the pan with plastic wrap and refrigerate for at least 4 hours to firm.

4 Holding the ends of the aluminum foil, lift the bar onto a cutting surface. Using a large, sharp knife, cut the bar into 48 pieces. Sift the confectioners' sugar over the top of the pieces. Store in an airtight container in the refrigerator for up to 2 days.

GLAZED CINNAMON STREUSEL BARS

These bars are all crunch: the bottom layer, spiced with cinnamon, is like a crisp butter cookie, and chopped pecans star in the toasted crumb topping.

FOR THE COOKIE CRUST

2 cups all-purpose flour

1½ teaspoons ground cinnamon

¼ teaspoon salt

1 cup unsalted butter, at room temperature

1 cup granulated sugar

1 large egg yolk

FOR THE TOPPING

¾ cup all-purpose flour

1 cup granulated sugar

½ teaspoon ground cinnamon

¾ teaspoon salt

½ cup cold unsalted butter, cut into ¾-inch pieces

1½ cups coarsely chopped pecans

Vanilla Glaze, page 104

MAKES 54 BARS

1 Position a rack in the middle of the oven and preheat to 325°F. Press a 20-inch piece of aluminum foil onto the bottom and over the sides of a 15½-by-10½-by-1-inch jelly-roll pan. Butter the foil.

2 To make the crust, in a bowl, sift together the flour, cinnamon, and salt; set aside. In a large bowl, combine the butter and sugar. Using a mixer on medium speed, beat until well blended, about 1 minute. Add the egg yolk and beat on low speed until the yolk is completely incorporated, scraping down the bowl occasionally with a rubber spatula. Slowly add the flour mixture and beat just until incorporated, about 30 seconds. Press the dough over the bottom and 1 inch up the sides of the prepared pan.

3 To make the topping, in another bowl, combine the flour, sugar, cinnamon, and salt. Using clean beaters, beat on low speed just to blend the ingredients, about 1 minute. Add the cold butter pieces and beat just until big (½–¾-inch) crumbs form. You will still see some loose flour. Stir in the pecan pieces and sprinkle the mixture evenly over the dough. Bake until the top is lightly browned, 40–45 minutes. Transfer to a wire rack to cool for 5 minutes. Cut into 54 pieces, then

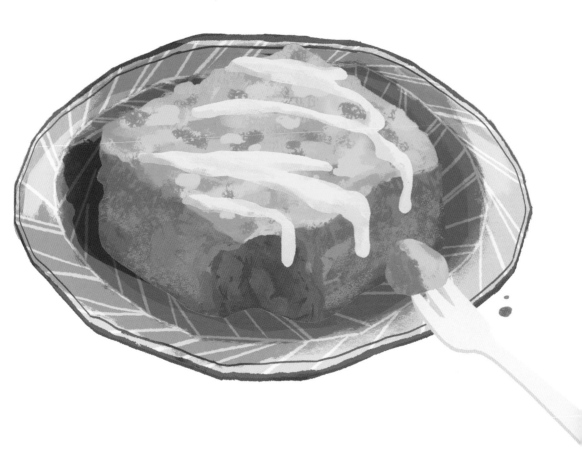

let cool until the top feels room temperature to the touch, about 1 hour.

4 Holding the ends of the foil, lift the cooled bars onto a cutting surface. Slide the bars apart to separate them slightly. Using a small spoon, drizzle the Vanilla Glaze over the crumb topping. Store the bars in an airtight container at room temperature for up to 4 days.

TART KEY LIME SQUARES

For a new twist on a classic bar cookie, try the unique flavor of Key limes instead of lemons. The skin of these small, round limes found in specialty-food stores is an attractive greenish-yellow.

1 Position a rack in the middle of the oven and preheat to 325°F. Press a 20-inch piece of aluminum foil onto the bottom and over the sides of a 13-by-9-by-2-inch baking pan. Butter the foil.

2 To make the crust, in a bowl, combine the flour, confectioners' sugar, zest, and salt. Using a mixer on low speed, beat just until blended, about 1 minute. Add the butter and beat until the largest pieces are the size of peas, 1–2 minutes. Press the dough over the bottom and 1 inch up the sides of the prepared pan. Bake just until the edges are lightly browned, about 20 minutes. Remove from the oven and set aside. Reduce the oven temperature to 300°F.

3 To make the filling, in a bowl, whisk the eggs just until blended. Add the granulated sugar and lime juice and zest and whisk until smooth, about 1 minute. Sift the flour into the bowl and whisk until incorporated. Slowly pour the filling over the crust. Bake until the filling looks set and does not wobble when the pan is shaken, 40–45 minutes. Transfer the pan to a wire rack and let cool until the top is room temperature, about 1 hour. Cover the pan with plastic wrap and refrigerate for at least 4 hours to firm.

4 Holding the ends of the foil, lift the bar onto a cutting surface. Using a large, sharp knife, cut the bar into 48 pieces. Store the squares in an airtight container in the refrigerator for up to 2 days.

FOR THE CRUST

1½ cups all-purpose flour

½ cup confectioners' sugar

1½ teaspoons grated Key lime zest

⅛ teaspoon salt

¾ cup cold unsalted butter, cut into ½-inch pieces

FOR THE FILLING

6 large eggs

2½ cups granulated sugar

¾ cup fresh Key lime juice

1 tablespoon grated Key lime zest

½ cup all-purpose flour

MAKES 48 SQUARES

BLUEBERRY CHEESECAKE BARS

These easy bars have all the elements of a traditional cheesecake: a graham cracker–crumb crust, rich creamy filling, and pockets of fresh fruit.

FOR THE CRUST

2¾ cups graham cracker crumbs

2 tablespoons granulated sugar

¾ teaspoon ground cinnamon

½ cup unsalted butter, melted

FOR THE FILLING

4 large eggs

1½ pounds cream cheese, at room temperature

1 cup granulated sugar

2 teaspoons vanilla extract

3 tablespoons all-purpose flour

½ cup sour cream

2 cups fresh blueberries

MAKES 48 BARS

1 Position a rack in the middle of the oven and preheat to 325°F. Press a 20-inch piece of aluminum foil onto the bottom and over the sides of a 13-by-9-by-2-inch baking pan. Butter the foil.

2 To make the crust, in a bowl, stir together the graham cracker crumbs, sugar, and cinnamon. Add the butter and stir until moistened. Press the crumb mixture over the bottom and 1 inch up the sides of the prepared pan. Bake until slightly darkened, about 10 minutes. Transfer to a wire rack and let cool slightly.

3 To make the filling, in another bowl, whisk the eggs just until blended; set aside. In a large bowl, combine the cream cheese, sugar, and vanilla. Using a mixer on medium speed, beat until well blended, about 1 minute, scraping down the bowl occasionally with a rubber spatula. Add the flour and beat just until incorporated, about 1 minute. Add half of the beaten eggs and beat just until evenly colored, about 30 seconds. Add the remaining eggs and beat just until blended. Add the sour cream and beat just until incorporated, about 30 seconds. Using a large spoon, gently stir in the blueberries. Pour the filling into the crust. Bake until the filling looks set and does not

wobble when the pan is shaken, 40–45 minutes. Transfer to a wire rack and let cool until the top is room temperature, about 1 hour. Cover the pan with plastic wrap and refrigerate for at least 4 hours to firm.

4 Holding the ends of the foil, lift the bar onto a cutting surface. Use a warmed knife to cut the bar into 48 pieces. Store the bars in an airtight container in the refrigerator for up to 3 days.

CARAMEL-GLAZED BLONDIES

These have the appealing texture of brownies, but the flavor comes from brown sugar instead of chocolate. Drizzling a rich caramel glaze over the top provides an extra layer of indulgence.

1 Position a rack in the middle of the oven and preheat to 325°F. Press a 15-inch piece of aluminum foil onto the bottom and over the sides of a 9-by-9-by-2-inch baking pan. Butter the foil.

2 To make the blondies, in a saucepan, combine the butter and brown sugar. Warm over medium heat, stirring, until melted and smooth. Scrape into a large bowl and let cool slightly. In a small bowl, sift together the flour, baking powder, and salt; set aside. Add the eggs and vanilla to the large bowl and mix until smooth. Stir in the flour mixture just until incorporated. Pour the batter into the prepared pan. Bake until a toothpick inserted in the center comes out with moist crumbs attached, 20–25 minutes. Transfer to a wire rack and let cool.

3 To make the glaze, in a saucepan, combine the butter, cream, and brown sugar. Warm over medium heat, stirring constantly, until melted. Increase the heat to medium-high and boil for 2 minutes. Remove from the heat and stir in the vanilla extract. Let cool. Sift the confectioners' sugar into a bowl, then whisk in the cooled brown sugar mixture to make a smooth glaze. Spread the glaze evenly over the cooled blondie in the pan. Let stand until set, about 30 minutes.

4 Holding the ends of the foil, lift the blondie onto a cutting surface. Use a warmed knife to cut it into 25 squares. Store the blondies in an airtight container in the refrigerator for up to 3 days.

FOR THE BLONDIES

½ cup unsalted butter

1½ cups firmly packed brown sugar

1½ cups all-purpose flour

1 teaspoon baking powder

¼ teaspoon salt

2 large eggs

1 teaspoon vanilla extract

FOR THE CARAMEL GLAZE

¼ cup unsalted butter

½ cup heavy whipping cream

¾ cup firmly packed dark brown sugar

1 teaspoon vanilla extract

½ cup confectioners' sugar

MAKES 25 BLONDIES

FROSTED CHOCOLATE BROWNIES

A high proportion of sugar and butter to flour and a good quantity of chocolate are what give these brownies their dense, dark texture. Use the highest-quality chocolate you can find.

¾ cup unsalted butter, at room temperature

5 ounces unsweetened chocolate, finely chopped

1 cup all-purpose flour

¼ teaspoon salt

4 large eggs

2 cups granulated sugar

1 teaspoon vanilla extract

Chocolate Frosting, page 105

MAKES 25 BROWNIES

1 Position a rack in the middle of the oven and preheat to 325°F. Press a 15-inch piece of aluminum foil onto the bottom and over the sides of a 9-by-9-by-2-inch baking pan. Butter the foil.

2 In a double boiler insert or large metal bowl that fits on the rim of a saucepan, combine the butter and chocolate. Place the insert or bowl on the saucepan over, but not touching, barely simmering water. Heat, stirring often, until the chocolate is melted and smooth, 3–4 minutes. Gently lift the bowl out of the pan and set aside to cool slightly.

3 In a small bowl, sift together the flour and salt; set aside. In a large bowl, combine the eggs and sugar and whisk to blend, about 45 seconds. Add the slightly cooled chocolate mixture and the vanilla and whisk until the mixture is evenly colored. Whisk in the flour mixture just until incorporated.

4 Pour the batter into the prepared pan. Bake until a toothpick inserted in the center comes out with moist crumbs attached, 30–35 minutes. Transfer to a wire rack and let cool until the top is room temperature, about 1 hour.

5 Holding the ends of the foil, lift the cooled brownie onto a cutting
surface. Using an offset spatula, spread the frosting evenly over
the top of the brownie. Use a warmed knife to cut the brownie
into 25 squares. Store the brownies in an airtight container in the
refrigerator for up to 3 days.

MARBLEIZED BROWNIES

Here, a rich cream cheese topping is swirled into classic chocolate brownie batter resulting in a marbleized bars for chocolate and vanilla lovers alike.

1 Position a rack in the middle of the oven and preheat to 325°F. Press a 15-inch piece of aluminum foil onto the bottom and over the sides of a 9-by-9-by-2-inch baking pan. Butter the foil.

2 To make the brownie batter, in a metal bowl that fits on the rim of a saucepan, combine the butter and chocolate. Place the bowl on the saucepan over, but not touching, barely simmering water. Heat, stirring often, until smooth, 3–4 minutes. Remove from the heat and let cool slightly. In a small bowl, sift together the flour and salt; set aside. In a large bowl, whisk the eggs and sugar until blended, about 1 minute. Add the chocolate mixture and the vanilla and whisk until evenly blended. Whisk in the flour mixture just until incorporated.

3 To make the cream cheese filling, in a bowl, stir together the cream cheese, sugar, egg, and vanilla until smooth.

4 Pour two-thirds of the batter into the prepared pan. Spoon the filling over the batter. Pour the remaining batter over the filling and, starting in 1 corner, swirl a spoon through the batter and filling to create a marble pattern. Repeat, starting from another corner. Bake until a toothpick inserted in the center comes out with moist crumbs attached, 35–40 minutes. Transfer to a wire rack and let cool. Holding the ends of the foil, lift the cooled brownie onto a cutting surface. Use a warmed knife to cut the brownie into 25 squares. Store the brownies in an airtight container in the refrigerator for up to 3 days.

FOR THE BROWNIE BATTER

½ cup unsalted butter, at room temperature

4 ounces unsweetened chocolate finely chopped

1 cup all-purpose flour

¼ teaspoon salt

3 large eggs

1¾ cups granulated sugar

1 teaspoon vanilla extract

FOR THE CREAM CHEESE FILLING

6 ounces cream cheese, at room temperature

¼ cup granulated sugar

1 large egg

1 teaspoon vanilla extract

MAKES 25 BROWNIES

VANILLA GLAZE

This versatile glaze, made by stirring together a few simple ingredients, is a great way to add extra flavor—or color—to your finished baked goods. Use it as an icing or for drizzling over cookies and bars.

1 cup confectioners' sugar

3 tablespoons heavy cream

½ teaspoon vanilla extract

a few drops food coloring, optional

MAKES ABOUT ½ CUP

1 Sift the confectioners' sugar into a small bowl. Add the cream and vanilla and stir until a glaze forms, about 1 minute. Add 1–2 drops of food coloring, if desired, and stir until uniform in color. For multiple colors, divide the glaze into small bowls and add different colors to each bowl.

2 To use the glaze, using a small icing spatula, spread the top of each cookie, brownie, or bar with a thin layer of glaze. Or, using a small spoon, drizzle thin lines of glaze over your treats.

CHOCOLATE FROSTING

Use this fluffy frosting to top brownies or to fill cookie sandwiches. Be sure to sift the confectioners' sugar first to avoid a lumpy consistency in the otherwise smooth and rich mixture.

2 ounces unsweetened chocolate, chopped

½ cup unsalted butter, at room temperature

1 cup confectioners' sugar, sifted

1 teaspoon vanilla extract

1 tablespoon heavy cream

MAKES ABOUT 1½ CUPS

1 Place the chocolate in a double boiler insert or a large metal bowl that fits on the rim of a saucepan. Place the bowl on the saucepan over, but not touching, barely simmering water and heat, stirring often, until the chocolate is melted and smooth, 3-4 minutes. Carefully remove the bowl from the heat and transfer to a work surface. Let cool until lukewarm to the touch, about 5 minutes.

2 In a large bowl, combine the butter and confectioners' sugar. Using a mixer on medium speed, beat until well blended, about 1 minute. Add the vanilla and beat until incorporated, scraping down the bowl occasionally with a rubber spatula. Add the cooled, melted chocolate and beat until the mixture is evenly colored. Add the cream and beat until the mixture looks fluffy, about 1 minute. Use as soon as possible. If the frosting sits too long and firms up, beat for 1 minute to return its fluffy character.

COOKIE FILLINGS

These thick fillings serve as a delicious "glue" for sandwiching two flat-bottomed cookies, such as macaroons, together. Vary the proportion of extracts if you want a stronger almond or vanilla flavor.

FOR THE ALMOND FILLING

⅓ cup confectioners' sugar

½ cup unsalted butter, at room temperature

½ teaspoon almond extract

½ teaspoon vanilla extract

FOR THE CHOCOLATE FILLING

⅓ cup heavy cream

1 tablespoon unsalted butter

4 ounces semisweet chocolate, finely chopped

½ teaspoon vanilla extract

MAKES ABOUT ¾ CUP EACH

1 To make the almond filling, sift the confectioners' sugar into a bowl. Add the butter and beat with a large spoon until the mixture is smooth and creamy. Beat in the almond and vanilla extracts until incorporated.

2 To make the chocolate filling, in a heavy saucepan over medium-low heat, combine the cream and butter. Heat until tiny bubbles form along the edges, about 2 minutes; do not let boil. Remove from the heat, stir in the chocolate, and let stand for about 30 seconds to soften. Stir in the vanilla and continue stirring until the chocolate is melted and the mixture is smooth. Let cool until thick enough to cling to an icing spatula, 30–45 minutes.

SWEETENED WHIPPED CREAM

You can use this lightly sweetened, vanilla-scented whipped cream for a variety of desserts. For the best results, put your bowl and mixer beaters in the freezer for about 30 minutes before whipping.

1 cup cold heavy cream

2 tablespoons confectioners' sugar

½ teaspoon vanilla extract

MAKES ABOUT 1½ CUPS

1 Pour the cold cream into a chilled bowl. Using a mixer on low speed, beat until slightly thickened, 1–2 minutes. Slowly increase the speed to medium-high and beat just until the cream holds a very soft (drooping) peak, 2–3 minutes.

2 Sprinkle the confectioners' sugar over the cream and add the vanilla. Beat until the cream holds firm peaks, 1–2 minutes longer. Watch carefully to avoid over-whipping the cream.

COOKIES

SHIPPING BAKED GOODS

Most cookies, brownies, and bars travel well if packed properly. Delicate cookies that break easily, those with frostings or fillings that could melt in hot weather, or the few that require refrigeration are not good candidates to ship. Cookies that can be stored without refrigeration for at least three days without losing any flavor are usually the best choices for mailing. Here are some helpful tricks to ensure your goodies get to their destination safely:

preparing to ship

- Wrap the cookies, brownies, or bars individually in plastic wrap.

- Line the bottom of a metal tin or rigid plastic container with a thick layer of crumpled waxed paper.

- Stack the wrapped cookies in the container, placing a piece of waxed paper between each layer.

- Pack the spaces between cookies with crumpled waxed paper.

- Seal the container tightly and secure the lid with tape.

packing the carton

- Select a carton large enough to hold the container with a few inches of space on all sides.

- Wrap the container carefully with plenty of packing material.

- Place the well-wrapped container in the carton, adding packing material all around.

- Enclose a note that lists the contents so that cookies are not accidentally thrown away with packing material and so the recipient knows the ingredients in the cookies (in case of allergies).

mailing the package

- Seal the carton with packaging tape, print the destination address clearly on a mailing label, and affix the proper postage.

- Ship the treats early in the week so they don't sit in a warehouse over the weekend.

- Choose a fast, reliable delivery method to ensure your baked goods arrive fresh.

INDEX

weldon**owen**

1045 Sansome Street, San Francisco, CA 94111

weldonowen.com

LITTLE TREATS: COOKIES

Copyright © 2018 Weldon Owen International
All rights reserved, including the right of
reproduction in whole or in part in any form.

Printed in China
First printed in 2018

10 9 8 7 6 5 4 3 2 1

Library of Congress
Cataloging-in-Publication data is available.

ISBN: 978-1-68188-428-8

WELDON OWEN INTERNATIONAL

President & Publisher Roger Shaw
SVP, Sales & Marketing Amy Kaneko

Associate Publisher Amy Marr
Senior Editor Lisa Atwood

Creative Director Kelly Booth
Art Director Marisa Kwek
Senior Designer Meghan Hildebrand

Production Director Michelle Duggan
Imaging Manager Don Hill

ACKNOWLEDGMENTS

Weldon Owen wishes to thank the following people for their
generous support in producing this book: Lou Bustamante and Elizabeth Parson.

Elinor Klivans is an award-winning pastry chef trained in France and the United States. She is the author of several cookbooks, including *Big Fat Cookies* and *Bake and Freeze Desserts*, a Julia Child Cookbook Award nominee, and a coauthor of Williams Sonoma *Essentials of Baking*. Klivans is also a frequent guest on radio and television and has written for numerous national magazines.

Clarisse Tanjo is an illustrator from Indonesia who loves creating whimsical, colorful scenes filled with cute characters, animals, and the delicious foods she has tried during her travels. She enjoys playing with colors and adding various patterns and textures to her illustrations. When Clarisse is not illustrating, you can find her in the kitchen, an apron tied at her waist, cooking and baking.